Daring Greatly

How the Courage to be Vulnerable Transforms the Way We Live, Love, Parent, and Lead

by

Brené Brown

A 30-MINUTE INSTAREAD SUMMARY

Please Note:

This is an unofficial summary. We encourage you to purchase the full-form book before or after reading the summary.

Book Overview

Daring Greatly: How the Courage to be Vulnerable Transforms the Way We Live, Love, Parent, and Lead is a book by Brené Brown. In this book Brown discusses scarcity in modern society. Modern media promotes the idea that no one is good enough. No one is beautiful enough, strong enough, or talented enough. There is always someone better. This creates an atmosphere in which people struggle with their own self-worth and the shame one feels when attempting to be vulnerable in a social situation.

There are many myths surrounding the idea of vulnerability. One myth suggests that vulnerability is weakness. However, the author uses an anecdote from her own life to express the idea that vulnerability can often lead to victory. In her example, she made herself vulnerable by delivering a public speech. The experience left her feeling deeply ashamed. However, it led to her speech being placed on a website and helping many people in their own struggles with vulnerability and shame.

Shame is a major reason why many people will not allow themselves to become vulnerable. Shame often originates in the societal expectations of gender roles. Women are expected to be small, sweet, and quiet. Men are expected to be strong. When men and women fight against these expectations, they are often filled with shame. The author, however, offers changes in thought processes that can help men and women deal with this shame and become shame resilient.

People often develop a persona, or type of armor to deal with the shame that comes with vulnerability. This armor is often the way people avoid vulnerability. They can numb their feeling with several methods or train themselves to dread joy because of the disaster that is likely to befall, eventually. The author offers multiple ways to deal with shame to allow them to drop their armor.

The author discusses the "disengagement divide", a gap between aspirational values and practiced values. She uses several examples to show the reader how people, most often parents, do not always practice what they preach, presenting a confusing example to those around them. This not only applies to parents or business leaders, but to community leaders as well.

There is often use of shame in organizations such as work environments and schools. This is meant to be a tool to encourage workers and students to work harder. However, it often backfires, causing students and employees to disengage in order to protect themselves from shame.

Finally, the author offers several suggestions as to how a parent can teach children to live "Wholehearted". To do this, the author says that parents must remember children learn by example. Therefore, parents must live a Wholehearted life and show children how to deal positively with shame and vulnerability. The author also suggests that parents must allow their children to struggle, because hope is taught in struggle.

List of Characters

Brené Brown: Brené Brown is the author of the book. She uses many examples from her own life and experiences while trying to live by the guidelines she has written about in her books about shame and vulnerability.

Steve: Steve is Brené Brown's husband. She often mentions her husband in the book when discussing her personal experiences involving shame and vulnerability.

Ellen: Ellen is Brené Brown's daughter. Brené Brown mentions Ellen multiple times in the book when discussing vulnerability and childhood.

Charlie: Charlie is Brené Brown's son. Brené Brown mentions Charlie when discussing vulnerability in childhood as well as in parenting.

Karen: Karen is a friend of Brené Brown's. She is mentioned several times when the author discusses the need for empathy when dealing with shame.

Chapter Summaries and Key Takeaways

What It Means to Dare Greatly

The author has always been inspired by Theodore Roosevelt's speech, "Citizenship in a Republic". The speech spoke of vulnerability and of trying, even if success is not guaranteed. To the author, this speech is about the reward of trying, not about winning or losing. It is for this reason that the author chose the phrase "Daring Greatly" for the title of this book.

Introduction: My Adventures in the Arena

The author is a social worker who specializes in research. She has previously done extensive research and writing on the topics of shame and living a Wholehearted life, a life filled with courage, engagement, and purpose. In doing this research, the author recognized problems in her own life that prevented her from following her own advice. One of these problems was a fear of being vulnerable. It reached a critical point in 2010 when the author was asked to speak at TEDxHouston, an independently organized event modeled after TED (Technology, Entertainment, and Design), a nonprofit organization devoted to "Ideas Worth Spreading." The author gave a speech in which she opened up about her personal life and allowed the audience to interact freely with her. She was surprised by the response she received at the event, and later when her speech was placed on the main TED website. This led to the author making many speeches about vulnerability, and those speeches became this book.

1: Scarcity: Looking Inside our Culture of "Never Enough"

Narcissism appears to be a worldwide epidemic. It is suggested that if people would only step back and look at the world in which they live, they would see that narcissism is just a symptom of vulnerability. It is people's way of dealing with the constant media assertion that an ordinary life is not good enough.

The author defines scarcity as "never enough". No one ever has enough money. No one is every successful enough. No one is ever beautiful enough. No one is ever what they want to be. This comes from a media-driven society that leaves people ashamed of who they are, people always comparing themselves to others, and people who disengage out of fear of not measuring up in a relationship. The opposite of scarcity is "Wholeheartedness", the author's description of what it is like to live a life in which you understand that you are enough.

2: Debunking the Vulnerability Myths

The author defines vulnerability as uncertainty, risk, and emotional exposure. Vulnerability is too often associated with dark, depressed feelings. It is often equated with failing and liability. It is about being emotionally naked. Even the author struggled with this sense of vulnerability when scheduled to give a speech at TEDxHouston. This sense of vulnerability was a result of the author having to force herself to come out of her comfort zone to speak with the audience in an honest and satisfying way. Many believe that being vulnerable leads to a dark and dangerous place. For the author, however, it led to victory rather than weakness. This debunks the myth that vulnerability is weakness.

Another myth the author has encountered in the past is the idea that some people never feel vulnerable. Quite often, people in positions of power, such as lawyers, doctors, and law enforcement officials, feel that they are above vulnerability. Their jobs force them to be confident so that vulnerability is less likely. However, the author insists that everyone is vulnerable at some point in their daily lives. Some just deal with it by denying it.

Some believe the only way to make a relationship work is to be completely vulnerable from the first date or meeting. This is not true. Vulnerability is not about putting yourself completely out there from the beginning of a relationship. It requires trust to feel vulnerable with another person, and trust is a slow, complicated process that requires work, attention, and full engagement of both parties.

No one can do everything alone. Vulnerability is not about being capable of doing everything without help. It is about asking for help. This is one of the things the author learned as she struggled on her own road to Wholeheartedness.

Key Takeaways

- Most people in modern society believe they are not good enough because the media suggests that an ordinary life is not desirable. This can lead to narcissistic-like behavior.

- There are many myths about vulnerability that are simply untrue. This includes the myths that vulnerability is weakness, that some people can choose not to be vulnerable, and the idea that you must be completely vulnerable in order to expect others to be vulnerable with you.

3: Understanding and Combating Shame

Shame is the fear of being vulnerable. When a person wants to share something they have created, whether it is a piece of artwork or an essay, fear will often lead them not to do it. If people dislike their piece of artwork or essay, it will forever be tied to the artist's sense of self-worth. On the other hand, if it is well-liked, the person will often fear not being able to live up to a standard.

There are three things everyone should know about shame: Everyone has it; everyone is afraid to talk about it; and, the less people talk about shame, the more control shame has over their lives.

There are three words with which shame is often interchanged in the modern vocabulary. One of them is "guilt". Shame is attacking oneself for not being good enough. Guilt is feeling bad for something done or something left undone. Shame is also interchanged with "humiliation". Humiliation is a response to someone else's attempt to shame. It is not internalized as shame is.

"Embarrassment", the final word often interchanged with shame in the modern vocabulary, is a feeling that passes, that might even be funny one day. It is a moment of unpleasantness. The person affected realizes it has happened to others, and therefore it is not symptomatic of a character flaw.

The author has studied shame extensively and has worked out many ways to battle it. The best way to battle shame is a method the author refers to as shame resilience. To do this, the author suggests a person go from shame to empathy, to learn to share shame with others. There are four ways to achieve this shame resilience. First, to recognize shame and understand its triggers. Second, to practice critical awareness. Third, the ability to reach out. And fourth, the ability to speak to others about shame. As an example, the author tells how she accidentally sent a mean email to a potential client in response to a cruel note. She dealt with the shame of this mistake by calling her husband and a friend, receiving two different reactions. The husband responded with a serious story of his own, similar mistake, and the friend with a funny story that helped the author to find humor in her mistake. This act gave voice to her shame. By doing so, it took the power from her shame.

Men and women both experience shame. Society expects women to be small, sweet, and quiet while using their time to make themselves pretty. Women are also expected to be perfect mothers or mother-figures.When women fight against these basic expectations, by taking high power jobs or choosing not to have children, they are often attacked and made to feel as though they are failing in some way. It is this that is the source of shame for most women. Society expects men to be strong. When a man shows any weakness, he is shunned. To illustrate this, the author tells the story of a young man whose uncle thought his work as an artist was too girly. The young man's parents made him stop drawing. Even many years later, this young man was emotionally affected by this episode and has never participated in making art again.

Women are also a big part of the problem for men when it comes to shame. Women ask men to be vulnerable, but when men are vulnerable women consider them weak. As an example, the author has spoken with many men who tell her that they refused to admit to their wives when they lost their jobs in fear that their wives would think them less of a man. Instead, they would leave their homes each morning and spend the day in a diner searching for a job via the newspaper or free wifi.

When faced with shame, most men respond in one of two ways: they rage or they shut down. One man admitted to picking an argument with his wife when he felt shamed by her admiration of the new home of a friend whose husband makes more money. Another admitted to feeling ashamed when his wife mentioned money more frequently after he turned down a higher paying job. For that reason, he stopped communicating with her as openly as he had before.

People tend to criticize others about things that fuel their own sense of shame. If a woman is ashamed of the way she looks, she might attack another woman who looks even worse than she does. This is a leading

cause of bullying, especially among children who are often repeating behaviors learned at home.

Another thing the author discovered during her research into men and their relationship with shame was that many men wrap their sense of self-worth into their sexuality. While most of the women the author interviewed admitted to being self-conscious of their looks during sex, most men the author spoke to admitted to feeling a sense of honor when a woman consents to having sex with them. Men often feel that when they are rejected in a sexual situation it is a reflection on their masculinity. This is true even when, intellectually, they understand the reason for the rejection.

The author also interviewed couples. In these interviews, she discovered it is in relationships that perpetrating shame becomes the most dangerous. People who love someone are witnesses to their deepest vulnerabilities. For this reason, it is these people who can do the most damage by pointing out those vulnerabilities. It is important for couples, parents, and other loved ones to learn how to express anger without perpetrating shame.

While both men and women experience shame, they experience it for different reasons. All these reasons, however, are based on societal expectations of what a man or a woman should be. Those who learn

shame resilience know this list of societal expectations. They learn to allow themselves to accept that they are not fulfilling those societal expectations and they are not bad people because of it.

Key Takeaways

- Shame is a feeling of inadequacy that all people experience, making it difficult for them to be vulnerable.

- Men and women feel shame because of societal expectations that dictate their behavior. For women, shame is often tied up to their appearance and their capability as mothers. For men, shame is most often about weakness and their perceived level of masculinity.

- Men and women often respond to shame in different ways. Men will rage or become withdrawn while women often shame others who suffer from the same inadequacies.

4: The Vulnerability Armory

Everyone develops some kind of persona, or armor, behind which they hide to protect themselves from vulnerability. Most people will remove this "mask" if they reach a specific point of "enough." That point could be finding enough worthiness within themselves, having enough (reaching a boundary), or knowing that it is enough to show up and take risks (engagement versus disengagement).

A piece of armor the author says people often adopt to avoid vulnerability is foreboding joy. People often look at joy as the calm before the storm. These people often feel better expecting the worst to happen, even when their life is filled with joy. The reason for this is to prevent being blind-sided by vulnerability. The antidote to foreboding joy is gratitude. The author suggests that readers who recognize in themselves a habit of expecting the worst in moments of joy should remember to be grateful for the person, the beauty, the connection, or simply the moment before them. The author discovered the connection between joy and gratitude through speaking with people who had experienced horrible tragedy. These people taught her that joy comes during everyday moments, that people should be grateful for what they have, and that they should not squander joy.

Another piece of armor people often adopt to avoid vulnerability is perfectionism. Perfectionism is an impossible goal that no one has ever attained. It is a self-destructive and addictive belief system that sets the person up for shame. The antidote to perfectionism is to learn to appreciate the beauty in the cracks, in other words, to find acceptance in their own flaws. The person who strives to be perfect has to learn to love themselves with their flaws, not in spite of them.

A final piece of armor people often adopt to avoid vulnerability is numbing. This could include anything from avoiding emotional situations to smoking to doing illegal drugs in order to avoid the shame that comes with vulnerability. The antidotes to numbing behaviors include learning how to feel emotion, staying mindful of numbing behaviors, and learning how to lean into the discomfort of hard emotions. The latter was the one idea that interested the author the most because it was the one she struggled with the most in her personal life. In her research, she learned that the most effective way to learn to lean into emotions was to set boundaries, to spend less time forging relationships that did not matter, and to maintain relationships that did.

Other types of armor include "Viking or Victim". This mentality takes on the idea that people will always become a victim at some point. Either a person lives their life always the Victim, always allowing others to take advantage of them, or they live their lives like a Viking, vigilantly, dominating others in an attempt to avoid becoming a victim. Many of these people work in high profile, high stress jobs, such as the law, finance, or the military. People with these types of jobs are susceptible to being a Viking or a Victim because of the highly competitive or combative atmosphere of these professions. Other Viking or Victim people include those who have experienced some type of trauma, whether it be abuse, combat, or neglect. By connecting with others to reintegrate with vulnerability and seek support, the author has witnessed changes in these types of people, especially when it comes to community outreach for members of the military.

Another type of armor is floodlighting. These are people who tend to overshare too early in a relationship, misusing vulnerability in a way that creates shame, either for the person oversharing or the person listening to the overshared emotions. The best antidote for floodlighting is to be clear on the motivation for sharing specific information. People should never share information that still causes them pain or that they are still working through emotionally. On the other end of the spectrum is the "smash and grab". This armor is a type of oversharing that manipulates vulnerability in an attempt at seeking attention. The same antidote to floodlighting is used to deal with smash and grab, with the added question of what specific need is driving the behavior.

Another type of armor is serpentining. It means trying to control a situation, backing out of it, pretending it's not happening, or even pretending not to care. Serpentining is a type of avoidance, similar to numbing. It also has aspects of disconnect, one of the biggest allies of shame. The antidote to serpentining is to be present, pay attention, and move forward.

Cynicism, criticism, cool, and cruelty are types of armor that can also be used as weapons. It is easy to criticize those who appear to be lesser than someone else, who do not look as good, do not work as well, or who do not seem to be as knowledgeable. To resist this type of armor, it is important to learn to walk the tightrope between constructive and destructive criticism. It is also important to understand whose opinion matters and whose does not.

5: Mind the Gap: Cultivating Change and Closing the Disengagement Divide

There is a debate over the difference between strategy and culture. Many believe that strategy is the most important thing in defining who a person is as an individual. Culture, to these critics, is simply the world in which the individual exists. To the author, however, these definitions are misguided. Instead, she defines strategy as "the game plan". She defines culture as who we are more than what we want to achieve. The author feels that culture is the most important issue in discussing behaviors because culture defines us, and understanding a specific culture helps when discussing change.

Disengagement is a basic problem in most families, schools, communities, and organizations. Disengagement is seen in everything from politics to religion. This leads to what the author calls the "disengagement divide", the gap between aspirational values (things we aspire to be and do) and practiced values (things that we are and do on a daily basis). It is not uncommon, especially for parents, to preach one set of values, but act in a totally different way. One example the author uses is a parent who teaches her children not to steal, but when she discovers the clerk at the grocery store forgot to ring up paper towels on the bottom of the cart, she does not return to the store to pay for them. People need to be careful that what they think and feel equates what they say and do.

Key Takeaways

- Most people use some kind of persona or armor to protect themselves from vulnerability.

- Some types of armor people use to protect themselves from vulnerability can also be used as weapons. People should be conscious of their motivations when criticizing others.

- The disengagement divide is the gap that sometimes exists between what a person thinks and feels and how they speak or act. It is important that people are aware of this gap and work towards closing it.

6: Disruptive Engagement: Daring to Rehumanize Education and Work

In her research, the author discovered that many people felt that when they put themselves out there to question ideas, they were often ridiculed. For this reason, many people stopped participating not only in the work environment but in school environments as well. The author realized that work and education have been dehumanized, and this must change in the modern world of scarcity.

Shame is not always obvious in a culture. When it is, it is an acute situation that needs to be dealt with swiftly. Some think of shame as a motivator. However, many people will begin to disengage in such an atmosphere in order to protect themselves from their feelings of shame. Shame is often seen in work atmospheres, such as the use of winner and loser lists or offering bonuses to the top achievers. Shame is often used in classrooms, not only in programs designed to encourage students to work harder, but also against teachers. In Texas, as well as other states, it has become common to shame teachers when state test scores are not as high as expected.

Shame and blame often go hand in hand. When someone feels shame, they often turn the blame on someone else in order to discharge their feelings or to hurt someone else. In an organization culture it is also common to find a cover-up in a shame situation. Organizations will often sacrifice the dignity of humanity in order to protect their reputation as an organization. Four strategies for fighting shame in an organization are: supportive leaders willing to dare greatly, finding and eliminating shame in the organization, making sure all leaders and managers are capable of letting employees know what is expected of them, and training all employees on the differences between shame and guilt.

Giving and receiving feedback in all social situations, from work to home life, is important. However, the exchange of feedback is often a highly vulnerable situation no matter what side a person is on. For this reason, many organizations and cultures avoid feedback. The exchange of feedback is a situation in which people need to learn to lean into difficult emotions and learn not to use their armor to protect themselves. People need to be able to relate to one another, to learn to recognize their faults as strengths, and to offer feedback in a way that engages with others rather than indulging in avoidance behaviors. For an example, the author talks of how she was taught during her social work training to speak with clients on the same side of the table. When a desk or table is placed between two people while sharing feedback, it can lead to a feeling of intimidation and shame. The author relates a time when one of her professors spoke with her about a paper she had written by sitting beside her, stressing the positives of the paper, and offering assistance in the publication of the paper. This turned a potential confrontation into a supportive discussion.

Vulnerability is necessary. Leaders need to be open to vulnerability in order to be effective in relating to their employees. Vulnerability is also an important part of creativity, innovation, and overall success.

7: Wholehearted Parenting: Daring to Be the Adults We Want Our Children to Be

Who we are and how we engage with the world are stronger predictors of how our children will do than what we know about parenting. As parents, we must show our children how to remove the armor of vulnerability and engage fully in relationships. Children learn by observing. When children learn shame, it changes who they are and how they relate to the world. Parents must not use shame as a parenting tool and teach children how to interact in a world filled with shame. Finally, parents must normalize the world for their children by sharing experiences that will help children see that they are not alone in their feelings and experiences.

There are a lot of different ways in which parents choose to raise their children. In order to embrace Wholeheartedness, parents must accept that there is not a right or wrong method of raising children. No one should feel that their method is wrong because someone else does not agree with it, but they also should not criticize someone who does things differently.

Another part of raising Wholehearted children is allowing them to know that they belong to the family unconditionally. Children need to know that there are no requirements placed on them to be a part of the family, that they do not have to meet certain expectations in order to receive love or to be fully engaged with other members of the family.

Children need to struggle in order to learn hope. For this reason, the most vulnerable moment for most parents will be the moment when they realize they must allow their child to struggle rather than have the parent step in to fix a difficult situation.

Final Thoughts

Fear, scarcity, and shame dominate the world. Daring greatly in such a world is not about winning or losing, but about courage. It is about living life fully instead of standing on the outside looking in.

Key Takeaways

- Feedback is a frightening thing for the giver and the receiver. However, it is a necessary vulnerability that allows people to turn shame into strength.

- In order to raise a Wholehearted child, parents must live their lives Wholeheartedly and show their children how to remove their vulnerability armor despite shame.

- Hope is learned through struggle. Parents must allow their children to struggle despite the vulnerability this act might cause.

A Reader's Perspective

Brené Brown's book, <u>Daring Greatly: How the Courage to be Vulnerable</u> <u>Transforms the Way We Live, Love, Parent, and Lead,</u> teaches its readers how to overcome the feelings of shame that often accompany acts of vulnerability. Shame is a feeling of inadequacy that can cause a person to have a physical reaction to moments of vulnerability. This book not only describes what causes shame, but also provides the reader with ways in which to deal with shame. The advice in this book can occasionally seem simplistic, but it can also be eye-opening if the reader is willing to open themselves to the ideas presented.

In a society that is so focused on oversharing and openly criticizing one another, this book offers practical ways in which to deal with the emotions tied up in these behaviors. The author shows the reader the times when proper use of vulnerability is an asset. Not everyone can hide from the real world, from the shame that comes hand-in-hand with living in a world of internet and social networks. It is impossible for someone to post anything on the internet and not be presented with criticism in some form. This book offers simplistic ways to handle such criticism.

The chapter on shame gives a fascinating look at what causes shame. The author describes societal norms that can often place stress on a person who does not always live up to the expectations for his or her gender. At the same time, the book allows the reader to see how the opposite sex sees themselves in society and why certain situations might cause them shame. It is also helpful for most readers to see how each gender responds to shame and how these responses can differ.

The author's discussion on parenting is one of the most interesting. The author suggests ways in which a parent might raise a Wholehearted child. The entire chapter takes most of the topics covered in earlier chapters and applies them to raising children. As with the majority of the book, these suggestions are simple and filled with common sense. The comment that "children learn by observing" is the most profound of this chapter, and should be the one thing all parents should remember.

Daring Greatly is a book about courage and the ability to live life to its fullest. The book teaches the reader to move past the shame placed on them by societal norms and push themselves to be the best they can be. It offers practical advice that is simplistic, but useful.

Thank you for purchasing this summary. We hope you enjoyed it. If so, please leave a review.

We are also interested in talking to you to learn how we can improve! Please email instaread.summaries@gmail.com to take a quick survey. We will send you a $5 gift card from the store of your choice upon completion of the survey! -:)

Made in the USA
San Bernardino, CA
28 September 2014